$\dfrac{1}{10}$

URAL OWL.
SYRNIUM URALENSE.

EX LIBRIS

The CLIC CELEBRITY COOKBOOK

ACKNOWLEDGEMENTS

The recipes in this book were generously donated to CLIC by their
famous contributors.

I am indebted to Anne Baker, who generously allowed the photographs for
this book to be taken in her splendid house.

The Registered Office of the CLIC Trust is:
CLIC House, ll/l2 Fremantle Square, Bristol BS6 5TL
Telephone: Bristol 248844

This book is for Edward

First published in 1989 by
Crawlands Publications,
Bratton Seymour,
Wincanton,
Somerset BA9 8BZ.

© Jennifer Harvey

ISBN 0-9514845-0-8

Line illustrations by Joanna Stevens
Photographs by Terence J. Donovan
Design and DTP by Graphic Examples, Sherborne
Printed in Great Britain by BPCC Paulton Books Limited

CONTENTS

FOREWORD

Her Royal Highness The Duchess of Kent, G.C.V.O.

Children who suffer from cancer or leukaemia show great courage in their fight against these diseases, often having to cope with years of painful treatment, hospitalisation and separation from their families and loved ones. The CLIC Trust provides enormous support not only to the young patients but also to their families.

The proceeds from the sale of this book will be used to continue "the fight for young lives" and the Trust is most grateful to you for your support.

Katharine

PATRON

Starters

THE RT HON

MARY, COUNTESS OF PEMBROKE & MONTGOMERY CVO, DL

WATERCRESS MOUSSE

8 oz Cream Cheese
7 oz Mayonnaise
1 Bunch Watercress
1 Sachet Gelatine
10 fl. oz. Stock
10 fl. oz. Cream (lightly whipped)
Seasoning

1. Put the cream cheese and the mayonnaise into a blender with the watercress leaves. Whizz. Season.

2. Add the gelatine, dissolved in the stock and whizz again.

3. Fold in the lightly whipped cream and pour into ramekin dishes.

4. Leave the mousse to set and then decorate with a few remaining watercress leaves.

5. Serve with triangles of brown bread and butter.

THE RT HON
BERNARD WEATHERILL PC, MP

Mr Speaker

SPEAKER'S HOUSE

WESTMINSTER

SW1A 0AA

Consomme Egg Starter

1 tin Campbells Consomme Soup

2 chopped hard boiled eggs

3 x 3oz packets of Philadelphia Cheese

1 teaspoon curry powder

Worcester Sauce

Garlic Salt

Pepper

1 packet of gelatine

Method

Chop the hard boiled eggs and place in the bottom of
a ramekin dish.
Liquidise the remaining ingredients and pour gently on
to the eggs.
Just before serving decorate with caviar or Danish
lumpfish, parsley and lemon slices.
Serve with brown bread and butter.

This is a delicious light starter and is quick and
easy to make.

It is practical, as it can be made well ahead of time
and can be placed on the table before the arrival of
the guests.

Bernard Weatherill

Speaker

11

HUBERT DOGGART MA

Cambridge, Sussex & England Cricketer, President MCC 1981-82

GREEN PIECES

(Starter for four - a la Hubert Doggart not Bamber Gascoyne!)

One Avocado
One Dessert Pear
One Kiwi Fruit
French Dressing

1. Peel and slice the fruit and arrange in alternate slices, encircling and overlapping.

2. Cover in a light French Dressing and decorate with black olives or pine nuts.

3. Serve chilled and ideally on white bone china.

"I like this starter because of it's differing textures and flavours. As well as it's appearance and taste, I also enjoy it's associations - avocado from Israel, where the Christian faith originated; dessert pear from Kent, Surrey, or Sussex, where Cricket was played in Tudor times; and Kiwi fruit, originally from the true antipodes."

DAVID SHEPHERD OBE, FRSA

Artist, steam train enthusiast

GARLIC MUSHROOMS

Button Mushrooms
One egg, beaten
Breadcrumbs
Small carton natural yoghourt
Clove garlic, crushed or garlic paste
Creamed stilton (optional)

1. For the dip mix together natural yoghourt, crushed garlic and creamed stilton. Put into individual dishes for each person.

2. Wipe the mushrooms and cut stalks off level with caps. Coat in egg and breadcrumbs and deep fry in oil until golden brown.

3. Serve immediately with the dip served separately.

(An alternative is to use a fondue pot with heated oil and let everyone fry their own mushrooms.)

"David Shepherd likes this dish as it is very tasty
and Mrs. Shepherd likes it because
it is very simple to prepare."

PRUE LEITH OBE

Restaurateur, Caterer, Author, Journalist

GOAT'S CHEESE FILO PARCELS ON SALAD

4 oz. Goat's cheese, skinned
8 Sheets filo pastry
Fat for deep-frying

Mixed salad leaves
Red apples
Walnuts

For the dressing:

1 tbs. Walnut oil
1 tbs. Salad oil
2 tsp. Lemon juice
Half a tsp. mild grain mustard
Salt and pepper

1. Cut the filo into 5" squares. Lay two together and use to enfold an ounce of cheese, drawing up the filo like Dick Whittington's bag. Pinch the neck of the bag together, but don't break the pastry round the cheese.

2. Heat the oil until a crumb will sizzle in it. Deep fry the parcels until brown and crisp. Drain well.

3. Make a salad with the leaves, apples (sliced or scooped-into-balls) and walnuts. Mix the dressing ingredients together, toss the salad in this and divide between four plates. Serve the hot parcels on top of the salad.

THE RT HON
MARGARET THATCHER MP

1O DOWNING STREET
LONDON SW1A 2AA

MYSTERY STARTER

Ingredients:

1 tin of beef consomme (undiluted)
2 packets Philadelphia cheese
1 flat teaspoon of curry powder

Method:

Pour a quarter of the tin of consomme into a
bowl and put into the refrigerator to set. Blend
the rest of the soup into the cheese until it is
really well mixed, and stir in the curry powder.

Put it into the refrigerator until set - at least
twelve hours. Serve in individual ramekins and
decorate with the jellied consomme already in
the refrigerator. Top each ramekin with a black
olive.

To vary this, left-over chicken, shrimps, or
mushrooms peeled (blanched in boiling water with
lemon juice), chopped and mixed with an addition
of fresh herbs available, may be added.

(This may be prepared a day in advance).

SERVES 4

PHILIP HAYTON
Newscaster

BAKED AVOCADO WITH BLUE CHEESE

For four people:

1. *Take 2 ripe avocado.*

2. *Heat the oven to 200C.*

3. *Slice avocado in half; remove stones.*

4. *Fill cavities with 1 oz. blue cheese each.*

5. *Place on baking sheet.*

6. *Bake for 20 minutes.*

7. *Serve hot with brown bread.*

"This recipe is actually my wife's favourite, but anything that gives her pleasure gives me pleasure."

THE HON
WILLIAM WALDEGRAVE MP

SMOKED TROUT PATE

2 Smoked Trout
225g Low fat cottage cheese, well drained
1 teaspoon Grated horseradish
Black pepper
Lemon juice

1. Skin and bone the trout.

2. If you have a food processor, all the ingredients can be pounded together. If not, mince the trout or chop very finely. Sieve the cottage cheese and beat in the smoked trout. Add the horseradish and the black pepper and lemon juice to taste.

3. Pile into a dish and refrigerate for three hours.

This pate is particularly good served with slices of smoked salmon, garnished with lemon wedges.

"I am fond of smoked trout and this is an excellent way of presenting it. It is also thoroughly healthy, which I am always being told by Caroline - not to say Edwina Currie - is important."

JANE ASHER
Actress

CRISPY POTATO SKINS

(Make plenty; these are always very popular. Cut into small pieces, they are excellent for a buffet.)

> **Several large potatoes, baked in the oven**
> **Butter**
> **Sour cream to serve**

1. Heat the oven to 400F/200C/Gas mark 6, or heat the grill to high.

2. Remove the flesh from the potatoes, leaving a thin layer of skin, and reserve for making another potato dish (see below). Spread the potato skins with butter, put them on a baking sheet and cook in the oven for 20 minutes, or under the grill for 5 -10 minutes, turning regularly, until they are crisp.

3. Serve immediately with the sour cream.

The potatoes can be cooked in advance.

RICE AND POTATO NUT BALLS

(A great way of using left-over cooked potato. They can be kept hot without spoiling and, made smaller, would be perfect finger food with a tomato sauce.)

> **1 lb. Cooked potato**
> **3 tsp. Butter, softened**
> **4 tbs. Double cream**
> **2 Egg yolks**
> **4 oz. Cooked rice**
> **4 oz. Finely chopped walnuts, or toasted sesame seeds**

1. Heat the oven to 350F/180C/Gas mark 4.

2. In a bowl, mash the potato to a puree, add the softened butter, cream and egg yolks. Mix well and add the cooked rice.

3. Shape the mixture into balls and roll each one in the walnuts or sesame seeds.

4. Cook the balls in the preheated oven for 15 minutes, and serve.

THE MOST REV & RT HON
ROBERT RUNCIE
Archbishop of Canterbury

SOUPE A L'ONION

1 lb. Onions
1 oz. Butter or dripping
1 oz. Flour
2 pints boiling water or vegetable stock
Seasoning
Bay leaf
Slices of French Bread
Grated Cheese

1. Finely chop the onions. Melt the butter in a thick pan and add the onions and brown slowly and well. (This will take at least 15 minutes.)

2. Dust in the flour, and pour on the boiling water or vegetable stock. Simmer for about half an hour, adding seasoning and the bay leaf.

3. Put several slices of French bread at the bottom of a casserole, pour on the boiling soup, first removing the bay leaf.

4. Dust thickly with grated cheese, then set the casserole in the oven for15-20 minutes to brown. Serve very hot.

ALAN BATES

Actor

ALAN BATES

April 18, 1989

Mrs. Jennifer Harvey
"Crawlands"
Bratton
Seymour
Wincanton
SOMERSET, BA9 8BZ

Dear Mrs. Harvey:

Thank you for your letter, and my apologies
for not replying before now, but I have been appearing
in IVANOV at the Strand Theatre, and rehearsing a second
play for some weeks now, so my correspondence has been
somewhat neglected.

I am often asked to contribute to cookery books,
and have now begun to decline, but as yours is such a
deserving cause, I give you below my favourite 'starter',
but must warn you that I have also given this to two
other similar books last year, so if you do not wish to
use it, I shall quite understand.

MELON SURPRISE
Ingredients:

1 ripe Honeydew (or other) Melon
Gin and sugar to taste.

Method:
Scoop out the flesh from the two
halves of the melon and cut into small cubes.
Marinate in the gin and sugar overnight in
refrigerator, then replace in the melon
to serve.

Good luck with the book

yours sincerely,

ALAN BATES

THE RT. HON.
TOM KING MP

SCALLOP AND SWEETCORN SOUP

1 Spanish onion, peeled and finely chopped
2 oz. Butter
2 Medium potatoes, peeled and finely diced
1 pint Chicken stock
Salt and freshly ground pepper
1 Small can sweetcorn
1/4 pint Milk
4 (or more) Scallops
2 Egg yolks
4 tbs. Double cream
Chopped chives or fresh parsley

1. Cook the onions in the butter until soft and transparent.

2. Add the potatoes and stir until all is buttery; cook very gently for about 15 minutes.

3. Add the chicken stock and simmer for about 15 minutes longer. Put through a liquidizer or a sieve.

4. Return to the pan and add salt and pepper to taste. Add the drained sweetcorn kernels and any liquid from the can and then the milk.

5. Add the scallops, chopped if very large, then stir in the egg yolks beaten up with the cream and let the soup slowly thicken without coming to the boil.

6. Scatter liberally with chives or parsley before serving.

CLIFF MORGAN CVO, OBE

Broadcaster

BROTH

8 Pieces stewing lamb
1 Large onion
2 Large carrots
2 Parsnips
1 Small swede
1 Large leek - or any other vegetable you fancy
3 Stock cubes

1. Dice the onion, and add to a knob of butter melted in a large saucepan. Cook for a few minutes and then add a pint and a half of water in which you have dissolved the stock cubes.

2. Add the meat and cook for an hour. Add the remaining vegetables, diced and cook for a further 30 minutes. Boil some potatoes separately.

3. Serve the Broth in bowls, and the meat and potatoes on a separate plate.

"The sort of life I lead does not lend itself to many scheduled meal times. I therefore fall back on one of the most simple of nourishing meals that was a regular when I was a boy living at home with my Mother and Father. It is a dish that can be made, and then re-heated when necessary. It is also inexpensive and easily prepared."

FELICITY KENDAL
Actress

WARM SALAD OF SMALL FRENCH BEANS

2 lbs. French Beans, young and freshly picked
Olive oil
Coarse salt, freshly ground pepper
Cold unsalted butter
Crusty white bread

The beans should be tiny and as freshly picked as possible. Snap off the tips, but leave them whole, and wash them quickly in cold water. Plunge them into a large quantity of well-salted water at a churning boil and cook, uncovered, at a continued rapid boil, until tender: 4 - 8 minutes approximately. Serve them, well drained, accompanied by the finest and freshest olive oil available, black pepper and salt, cold unsalted butter, and rough crusty white bread. The contact of the olive oil with the hot beans produces a delicious explosion.

"This recipe is from THE FRENCH MENU and I particularly like it because of its simplicity - it doesn't clash with any main course."

JONATHAN DIMBLEBY

Broadcaster, Journalist & Author

**N E W S &
C U R R E N T
A F F A I R S**

BRITISH BROADCASTING CORPORATION
ON THE RECORD
11MF GROVE STUDIOS
LONDON W12 7RJ
TELEPHONE 01 576 7927
FAX 01 740 8549

Ms Jennifer Harvey
CLIC House
11-12 Fremantle Square
Cotham
Bristol BS6 5TL

4th May 1989

Dear Jennifer Harvey,

I am quite involved myself in the work of cancer research and relief and I am delighted to contribute a little towards your Trust.

My favourite first course is sliced tomatoes with mozzarella cheese. It is simple to make , delicious, especially on a hot Summer day and cheap (and if you want cheaper you can leave out the mozzarella).

The ingredients are fresh tomatoes, salt, pepper, sugar, mozzarella cheese, olive oil, vinegar and fresh basil.

Instructions:

(1) Finely slice tomatoes and place in a shallow dish.

(2) Mix oil and add vinegar, dressing to taste (but oily rather than vinegary).

(3) Chop basil, slice mozzarella cheese.

(4) Intersperse mozzarella slices with the tomatoes in dish.

(5) Sprinkle salt, pepper and basil to taste , add tiny amount of sugar (half a teasp).

(6) Add oil and vinegar dressing.

(7) Marinate for ten minutes.

(8) Eat with fresh brown crusty bread - and you will need no main course.

Yours sincerely

Jonathan Dimbleby

24

Main Courses

HER ROYAL HIGHNESS
THE DUCHESS OF GLOUCESTER

MUSHROOM ROULADE

Souffle

1 oz Butter
1 oz Flour
10 fl.oz. Milk
4 Eggs
3 oz Grated Cheese
Seasoning

Filling

1oz Butter
1 oz Flour
5 fl.oz. Milk
5 fl.oz. Chicken Stock
4 oz. Mushrooms
3 oz Lean Back Bacon

1. Grease and line 13" x 9" baking tray.

2. For the souffle, melt the butter, add the flour and cook for 2 minutes.

3. Remove from the heat, add the milk, return to the heat, bring to the boil stirring constantly and cook for 4 minutes.

4. Off the heat add the cheese, egg yolks and seasoning.

5. Beat the egg whites until stiff and fold into the cheese sauce.

6. Pour the mixture into the prepared tin and bake at Gas 4/180C/350F for 15 minutes.

7. Meanwhile, make the filling: melt 1 oz. butter and make the sauce as before, using the milk and stock.

8. Melt the remaining butter in a saucepan, cook the chopped bacon for 2 minutes, slice the mushrooms, add them to the bacon and cook slowly until tender. Add to the sauce.

9. Remove the souffle from the oven, cover with a clean tea towel then turn the tin over so that the souffle comes out. Leave for five minutes.

10. Spread the filling over the souffle, leaving a 1" margin around the edges. Roll up like a swiss roll. Serve hot.

THE RT. HON.

JOHN MORRIS QC, MP,

Labour Spokesman for Legal Affairs

PORK CHOPS WITH PINEAPPLE

4 Pork Chops
1 Small tin pineapple slices
1 Medium onion
1 tbs. Tomato puree
1 tsp. Thyme - dried, or fresh
1 dsp. Plain flour
Freshly milled black pepper
Salt

1. Brown the chops in a heavy frying pan using as little oil as possible. Transfer to casserole and place pineapple slice on each.

2. Add flour to the juices in frying pan. Slowly add the liquid from the pineapple and the tomato puree. Stir whilst bringing to the boil - it may be necessary to add a little water if mixture is too thick and likely to become lumpy.

3. Add finely chopped onion, the thyme, salt and pepper. Pour sauce over the chops and cook in the oven for around 40 minutes at 375F or 190C until chops are cooked.

4. Serve with baked potatoes and a green salad.

NICHOLAS WITCHELL
Newscaster

SPAGHETTI CARBONARA

10 oz. Smoked Back Bacon, cut into matchstick-sized strips
1 oz. Butter
3 tsp Olive Oil
4 oz. Parmesan Cheese or grated mature cheddar cheese
Black pepper
Tarragon
3 Cloves of garlic
2 Egg yolks
1 Egg white
1 Glass dry white wine
1 Small carton of single cream
8 - 12 oz. Spaghetti

1. Crush the garlic slightly and saute until light yellow, then add three tablespoons of olive oil.

2. When lightly golden remove the garlic from the oil and discard; add the bacon along with 1 oz. butter. Remove pan from heat.

3. Cook the pasta in lightly salted boiling water; warm serving dish.

4. When the pasta is cooked Al Dente (just cooked), replace the pan with the bacon and reheat so that the bacon becomes crisp.

5. Take the warm serving dish and add the cheese, cream and eggs and mix until a smooth sauce. Add the herbs and seasoning.

6. Into the dish pour the strained pasta and mix with the sauce; add the reheated bacon, together with the oil, and mix well.

7. Serve immediately, with a crisp green salad.

PADDY ASHDOWN MP

ALICE'S PACIFIC PIE

1 Tin tuna fish
1 Tin condensed mushroom soup
1 Tin sweetcorn (drained)
3 Packets "Chicken Flavoured" crisps
4 oz. Grated cheese

1. Butter a souffle dish and line with one packet of crushed crisps.

2. Mix together the tins of tuna fish, soup and sweetcorn.

3. Put a layer of the fish mixture into the souffle dish and then add some crisps; repeat the layers finishing with crisps and top with grated cheese.

4. Put pie into moderate oven for 30 minutes. Serve with a salad.

"I like it because it's tasty, and also because it's quick and easy but tastes complicated and very good!"

THE RT HON
THE EARL OF HAREWOOD KBE

GRILLED CHICKEN

One chicken quarter for each person
Watercress

1. Pre-heat the grill to a medium heat, and place the chicken quarters bone side up under the heat. Cook gently and steadily for at least 20 minutes, without turning the chicken over. Baste regularly with the juices as they run from the bird - no additional fat is necessary but the constant basting is very important.

2. Five minutes before serving, reverse the chicken so that the skin side is up, raise the heat, baste well and grill until the chicken skin is crisp and bubbling.

3. Serve immediately, garnished with watercress, and accompanied by a green salad.

This recipe is a particular favourite of Lord Harewood's - it is very simple to do, is nourishing and he thinks his wife does it better than anyone else!

——— **Typical Menu for a Dinner Party at Harewood House** ———

Cold Jellied Bortsch with soured cream

Roast Black Lamb with garlic and corriander
Buttered cauliflower with slivered almonds
Mange-toutes

Lemon Sorbet

VIRGINIA LENG MBE

International Three Day Event Rider, Olympic Silver Medalist

The P & N Company

TROUT MOUSSELINE with Prawn Sauce!

8 oz trout skinned + boned
1 whole egg
1 egg white
3/4 pt. Double Cream
Melted butter, salt + pepper.

Blend the trout with seasoning in
blender for 3 mins. Add whole egg
+ egg white - blend. Put mixture
in the fridge for 30 mins. to firm up.
Return to mixer + add cream. blend.

Sauce.
Mix 1oz butter with 1 level tblspoon
of flour then gradually add the
1/2 pt. milk. 4oz prawns tom puree
(1 teaspoon) eggs yoke + heat
slowly.

VAT REGISTRATION NO : 484 7886 76
Virginia Leng trading as the P & N Company

31

LOUISE BOTTING
Broadcaster & Financial Journalist

LOUISE BOTTING'S SALAD

"My favourite meal these days is WARM SALAD. All it consists of is: some mixed green salad (crispy lettuce, lambs leaves, chicory, endives, watercress etc.) tossed in a light French Dressing and sprinkled with fresh herbs from the garden.

Just before eating add your cooked ingredient hot from the pan. Sauted scallops with toasted pine kernals are good. Chicken livers are cheap and tasty. Bite sized pieces of chicken breast, marinated in soya sauce, fresh ginger, garlic and marmalade then fried are always popular. For vegetarians try green lentils soaked for a couple of hours and boiled for five minutes or so, so they are still crunchy. Add fried sliced garlic cloves and chopped spring onions, salt and freshly milled pepper.

Experiment yourself with anything your family find tasty. You can arrange the salad on plates before the guests are sitting at the table but only add the hot ingredients right at the last minute."

'Watercress Mousse'. Recipe page 10.

JULIAN LLOYD WEBBER
Cellist

DUCK WITH CHERRIES AND KIRSCH

1 Duck (approx. 5 lb.)
Salt and black pepper
1 oz. Unsalted butter
4 fl. oz. Kirsch
16 oz. Tin morello or black cherries
Lemon juice
5 fl. oz. Port
3 Level tsp. cornflour
Chopped parsley

1. Joint the duck into four equal portions and prick the skin thoroughly with a darning needle. Season with salt and freshly ground pepper.

2. Melt the butter in a large saute pan and fry the duck over a low heat for about 20 minutes or until brown all over.

3. Drain the fat from the pan and pour over the duck the kirsch and the juice from the cherries. Bring the contents to simmering point, cover the pan tightly with a lid and continue simmering the duck for 45 - 55 minutes.

4. Lift the duck portions from the pan, drain on crumpled absorbent paper and keep them warm.

5. Skim as much fat as possible from the pan juices and stir in the port.

6. Mix the cornflour with 2 tbs. of cold water, and stir into the pan juices until thickened. Bring to the boil and adjust seasoning; add the cherries and heat through.

7. Arrange the duck portions, coated with the sauce, on a dish. Sprinkle with parsley.

"I like this dish because it is good tasty English cooking."

RON MOODY
Actor

DE LUXE SALMON SALAD

8 oz. Tin pink salmon (drained)
4 oz. Curd cheese
1 Small onion (finely chopped)
Salt and pepper
Smoked salmon, 2 slices per person (or more)

1. Chop up onion, and mix it into the curd cheese. Mash up the pink salmon and add to the onion and cheese mixture. Add salt and pepper to taste. Mix all ingredients thoroughly.

2. Arrange a choice of salads on the plate, for example: Carrot and coconut; apple, date, walnut and celery; mixed bean; tomato, cucumber, lettuce and radish.

3. Leave the centre of the plate clear and put the salmon mixture in the middle with the smoked salmon over the top. (The salmon mixture is marvellous served on its own with brown toast.)

"I can barely boil an egg, but I have a wife who not only cooks but also believes in healthy meals. One of our favourite recipes is the Salmon Salad (Therese has graded it De Luxe) which is probably because of the contrast of the two textures of salmon and the varied salads. We both wish you enormous success with your book to aid such a vital cause."

'Scallop & Sweetcorn Soup'. Recipe page 21.

36

CLARE FRANCIS MBE

Yachtswoman, Author

VEGETABLE LASAGNA

1 Green pepper
1 Large onion
8 oz. Mushrooms
1 lb. Aubergines
Grated carrots   )
8 oz. Courgettes)   optional
6 - 8 oz. Lasagna
1 Tin tomatoes
Tomato puree
10 fl. oz. Stock
1 Tin kidney beans
Salt and pepper
Herbs/fresh basil if available
Bechamel sauce
Grated cheese

1. Gently cook onion, peppers and mushrooms for about 10 minutes, plus carrots if you wish. Meanwhile, steam aubergines and courgettes for about 10 minutes; add tomato puree to the fried vegetables and mix well.

2. Add drained kidney beans, tomatoes and freshly steamed vegetables. Stir gently and simmer for 5-10 minutes.

3. Take freshly cooked pasta (or pre-cooked variety) and, starting with the bechamel sauce, alternate with layers of pasta, vegetables and sauce, finishing with layer of sauce.

4. Top the dish with grated cheddar or mozarella cheese. Cook in the oven for 20 - 25 minutes at Gas Mark 6.

DAVID GOWER
Cricketer

BEEF WELLINGTON

3 lbs. Fillet of Beef
4 oz. Pate
8 oz. Mushrooms - finely chopped
1 lb. Puff pastry (or shortcrust)
Beaten egg to glaze
Salt, pepper and 1 tbs. oil

1. Pre-heat oven to 230C/425F. Rub the beef with salt, pepper and oil. Roast on a rack for 40 minutes. Remove and leave to cool.

2. When cool, cover the top and sides with the pate and chopped mushrooms.

3. Roll out the pastry thinly, large enough to envelope the meat. Put the fillet top side down on the pastry, and enclose into a parcel sealing the ends. Turn meat seam-side down, and decorate with spare pastry if you can be bothered! Glaze with the beaten egg.

4. Bake for a further 40 minutes or so, until the pastry is golden brown and puffed up. (Tastes even better if served with a red wine sauce.)

"Shouldn't be hungry after all that!"

MARK HARRINGTON

Head Chef, Ston Easton Park, Nr. Bath

ROAST MONKFISH TAIL WITH SPINACH NOODLES
IN A VERMOUTH AND SAFFRON CREAM

4 - 6 oz. Monkfish tails, on bone
2 pints Fish stock
1 glass Vermouth
Saffron Powder
8 Shallots, chopped
1 Sprig thyme
1 Spring Tarragon
10 fl. oz. Double cream
Salt and pepper
8 oz. Spinach noodles

1. Place chopped shallots into a sauteuse pan and sweat off.

2. Add vermouth and fish stock and reduce to approximately 5 fl. oz.

3. Add double cream, saffron powder, tarragon and thyme and simmer until sauce coats the back of a wooden spoon. (This is done by reducing the sauce.)

4. Liquidise the sauce and pass it through a fine strainer. Season to taste with salt and pepper.

5. Trim Monkfish tail of any skin but leave on bone.

6. Heat up saute pan with a little butter or oil and add Monkfish to pan, and brown lightly on each side.

7. Put fish into hot oven for about 8 minutes (depending on size of monkfish). Remove from oven and rest in a warm place for 5 minutes.

8. Cook the noodles in boiling salted water and drain. Take Monkfish off the bone by running a sharp knife along the bone the full length of the fish. Slice fish and arrange neatly around the noodles. Pour the sauce around the fish and serve.

JUNE WHITFIELD
Actress

BEEF STEW

This is best cooked a day ahead and is good for weekend visitors.   It is a one-dish
meal and freezes well but add vegetables when defrosted.

1. Cut into small pieces: *8oz. Salt pork or streaky bacon*

2. Cut into stewing pieces and remove fat and gristle:

   24 oz. Chuck steak
   8 oz. Shin

3. Into a plastic bag put *1 tbs. flour, 1 tsp. salt, pinch of pepper.*
   Put the meat into the bag and shake it to coat meat with flour mixture.

4. Saute the pork or bacon slowly and brown the meat in dripping over a quick
   flame.

5. Combine and heat until boiling:

   1 Clove garlic, chopped
   1 large onion, chopped
   1 Stock cube dissolved in a cup of hot water
   8 oz. Tin of tomatoes
   Small tin tomato puree
   12 Peppercorns
   3 Whole cloves
   2 tbs. Chopped parsley
   1 Bay leaf

6. Put the meat into a clean casserole and pour over the ingredients above.
   Cover, and simmer for 4 hours.   After 3 hours add half a cup of sherry or dry
   white wine.

7. Cook separately:

   6 Potatoes, medium size
   6 Carrots, peeled and quartered
   1 Stick celery, chopped

(Add these cooked vegetables to the casserole fifteen minutes before serving.)

'Beef Stew'. Recipe page 40.

JENNI MILLS
Broadcaster

SALMON EN CROUTE

"I don't eat much meat, but I love fish - and salmon is positively my favourite when I'm cooking for guests. I cook it this way because it looks amazingly posh, and everybody who comes thinks it must be terribly difficult - in fact it's really easy. It should serve 4 to 6 people, depending on how greedy they are. But I have to say that however big a bit of salmon I use I've never managed yet to end up with any leftovers to eat cold the next day".

2 - 3 lbs. Salmon tail, filleted into two pieces and skinned
1 lb. Puff pastry
2 oz. Butter
8 oz. Button Mushrooms, finely chopped
2 tsp. each : Fresh tarragon, parsley, dill, finely chopped
1 tsp. Grated lemon rind and 2 tsp. Lemon juice
A slurp of white wine to give you an excuse to open the bottle
Salt and freshly ground black pepper
Beaten egg

1. Melt the butter in a pan and add the chopped mushrooms; cook gently for 5 minutes. Add the herbs, lemon juice, lemon rind, the slurp of wine, and salt and pepper to taste - cook for 2 minutes more.

2. Roll out half of the pastry thinly, and an inch bigger all round than the fish. Lift it carefully onto a large dampened baking sheet. Put one of the filleted halves of salmon onto it.

3. Cook the mushroom mixture then spread it on top of the salmon and place the other fillet on top. Trim the pastry to that it's an inch bigger all round than the fish, and brush the edge with beaten egg.

4. Roll out the rest of the pastry to a similar size and thickness, and lay it over the fish. Press the edges together with a fork, and trim off any excess.

5. Now for the artistic bit: mark pretend fish scales on it in an over-lapping pattern, using the top edge of a teaspoon. Brush the whole fish with beaten egg.

6. Bake it in a preheated oven, Gas mark 7/220C/425F for 20 minutes. Turn the oven temperature down to Gas Mark 3/160C/325F and cook for a further 20 minutes or so, until the pastry is golden.

7. Serve garnished with sprigs of dill and cucumber slices.

Puddings

FAY WELDON
Writer

MARY GOWING'S PUDDING

"There is a kind of memorial pudding I make; the memorial being, in my head, to a former friend and colleague in an advertising agency in which I worked - a certain Mary Gowing. She was in charge of the Egg Marketing Board advertising in the sixties and died suddenly, mid-campaign, leaving me, the merest apprentice, to take over. One of her recipe advertisements in the "Add an Egg" series went: "Add four eggs and it cuts like a cake" and the phrase runs through my head whenever I make a Creme Caramel. It's so easy.

 Thus: 6 tablespoons sugar browned in six tablespoons of water. (Watch it - brown it, DON'T burn it. Seconds make a difference). That makes the caramel. Pour into the bottom of a flattish glass oven dish - a flan dish does very well. Beat up four eggs in a pint of milk, sweeten slightly, add vanilla if you like it (purists steep a vanilla pod in the milk first). Pour the mixture over the caramel, and bake in a slow oven for an hour or so, until set - until, indeed, it "cuts like a cake". Too hot and the mixture separates and becomes a little watery; too soon and it's runny; too long and it tends to get hard - but it's servable and delicious even it it's less-than-perfect form.

So if you do chose to make a creme caramel, remember, as I do, Mary Gowing. She worked for the Ministry of Food in the war, when the first few brave steps in bringing the public out of total nutritional ignorance and into knowledge were taken. In five short years we turned from an unhealthy to a healthy nation. She did not marry - the war took so many young men - and had no children, but left wisdom behind instead. And that's really something!"

LINDA McCARTNEY

Photographer & Singer

APPLE SAUCE CAKE

4 oz. Butter or margarine
4 oz. Sugar
1 tsp. Vanilla essence
1 Egg, beaten
12 fl. oz. Apple Sauce
8 oz. Plain flour

2 tsp. Bicarbonate of soda
Pinch of sea salt
5 oz. Broken pecan nuts
6 oz. Mixed dried fruit, chopped
Ground cinammon - good pinch
Ground nutmeg - good pinch

1. Pre-heat the oven to 350F/180C (Gas Mark 4), and lightly grease and flour an 8" cake tin.

2. Cream the butter and sugar together in a mixing bowl. When fluffy gradually add the vanilla and egg, beating thoroughly after each addition. Mix in the apple sauce.

3. Sift the flour, bicarbonate of soda and salt together into a separate bowl. Add the remaining ingredients to the flour mixture and stir well.

4. Stir the dry mixture into the creamed mixture to make a smooth batter. Transfer to the prepared cake tin, spread evenly and bake for 1 hour.

TO MAKE THE APPLE SAUCE :

1 lb. Apples, peeled and chopped
5 fl. oz. Water
1 tsp. Chopped lemon peel
Cinnamon (good pinch)
4 tbs. Sugar (optional)

1. Put all the ingredients together in a pan, just cover with water and bring to the boil. Reduce the heat and simmer, stirring occasionally, until the sauce has thickened.

2. Sweeten with sugar if desired.

   Serve hot or cold, with or without custard.

"My favourite because it is easy to make, very tasty, and can be eaten hot or cold."

BARBARA CARTLAND

Authoress

ICE CREAM LOAF

1 oz Butter
3 Eggs
4 oz. Fruit Sugar
2 oz. Ginger Biscuits, crushed
10 fl.oz. Double Cream
Zest and Juice of 1 orange
Zest and juice of 1 lemon
2 oz. Flaked Almonds - toasted

1. Prepare a 2 pint loaf tin by buttering the sides and base with the butter. Sprinkle the sides and base with the ginger biscuit crumbs to coat it all as evenly as possible.

2. Separate the eggs, and whisk the whites until they reach the soft peak stage. Gradually whisk in the sugar about l oz. at a time, until the meringue mixture is thick.

3. Whisk the cream up well with the egg yolks. Using a metal spoon, fold the meringue mixture into the egg-and-cream mixture, followed by the orange and lemon juice and grated zest. Fold in the flaked almonds.

4. Pour the mixture into the loaf tin and put in the freezer overnight.

5. Remove from freezer an hour or so before serving. Turn out by placing the base of the tin in hot water for a few seconds and ease the ice-cream loaf out with a palette knife.

6. Decorate with thin slices of orange and lemon cut into halves.

7. Serve cut into slices.

PAUL SCOFIELD CBE

Actor

POTATO PUDDING

1 lb. Potatoes (when peeled)
3 oz. Sugar
3 oz. Butter
4 Eggs
Grated rind of one lemon
Pinch of Salt

1. Boil potatoes and mash smooth and dry.

2. While still hot, beat in butter, sugar, eggs and salt.

3. Bake in a moderate oven for 40 minutes and serve sprinkled with either sugar or a preserve.

"I like this pudding because it is surprising that potato makes such a delicious dessert."

RUTH RENDELL
Writer

CHOCOLATE STRAWBERRY LOG

"This isn't exactly my favourite pudding. It's a pudding I like and is very, very easy to make. My favourite would be some fabulous cheesecake or Black-Forest-style confection, strictly to be selected from the sweet trolley in a restaurant. Such things I am incapable of making, lacking the time, the patience, and, alas, the expertise. Puddings I love, as I believe most vegetarians do, though I try to discipline myself not to indulge too often. This one looks rather splendid, doesn't have to be cooked and could certainly be put together by an artistic seven-year-old."

2 Packets ginger biscuits, the kind called gingernuts
Half a pound of strawberries or small tin of strawberries
Castor or icing sugar to taste
Large wineglass of sweet sherry or strawberry juice
Half pint double cream
Small bar of milk chocolate, grated

1. Soak the biscuits in the sherry or strawberry juice.

2. Mash or blend half the strawberries, adding sugar if they are the fresh kind, and mix with half the stiffly whipped cream.

3. Take the biscuits from the liquid, spread each one on each side with strawberry cream, and arrange them in a dish as if they were in the packet, log-wise that is, sandwiched by the strawberry cream.

4. Cover the log with the remaining cream, decorate with the remaining strawberries and sprinkle with the grated chocolate.

'Chocolate Strawberry Log'. Recipe page 48.

NED SHERRIN
Producer, Director, Writer & Presenter

SUMMER PUDDING

6 - 8 Slices stale, crustless thick white bread
24 oz. Mixed soft fruits
4 oz. Caster sugar

Strawberries, raspberries, red and black currants, as well as black cherries, are all suitable for this dish.   The more varied the fruits, the tastier the result - but don't use too many blackcurrants as their colour will dominate the pudding.

1. Line the bottom of a one and a half pint souffle dish or pudding bowl with one or two slices of bread, to cover the base completely. Line the sides of the dish with more bread, cut to shape, so that the bread fits closely together.

2. Hull and carefully wash the fruit and put in a pan and sprinkle the sugar over it. Bring to the boil over a very low heat and cook for 2 - 3 minutes only until the sugar melts and the juices begin to run.

3. Remove the pan from the heat and set aside 2 tablespoons of the fruit juices. Spoon the fruit and the remaining juice into the prepared dish and cover the surface closely with the rest of the bread.

4. Put a plate that fits the inside of the dish on top of the pudding and weight it down with a heavy tin or jar. Leave the pudding in the refrigerator to chill for 8 hours.

5. Before serving, remove the weight and plate; cover the dish with the serving plate and turn upside-down to unmould the pudding. Use the reserved fruit juice to pour over any parts of the bread which have not been soaked through and coloured by the fruit juices.

6. Serve with a bowl of lightly whipped cream.

"This is my favourite pudding because it requires almost no cooking and it is the only one I can do."

EDWINA CURRIE MP

PASSION CAKE

8 oz Wholemeal Flour
1 level teaspoon baking powder
Pinch Cinnamon
6 oz Grated Carrot
6 oz Soft Margarine
6 oz Soft Brown Sugar
Zest and Juice of one orange
3 Eggs
2 oz Walnuts (chopped)
1 fl. oz. Semi-Skimmed Milk

3 oz Margarine
12 oz Low Fat Soft Cheese
3 oz Icing Sugar
2 oz Walnut Halves

1. Mix together flour, baking powder, cinnamon and carrot.

2. Cream together margarine, sugar zest and orange juice. Gradually beat in eggs.

3. Add flour mixture and walnuts.

4. Mix, adding milk for a soft consistency. Divide into lightly greased 9" tins.

5. Bake at l80C/350F, Mark 4 for 30 minutes, until well risen and golden brown.

6. Cream margarine and then mix in cheese and icing sugar.

7. Sandwich cooled cakes with two thirds of the topping and spread remainder on top and decorate with walnut halves.

Nutritional Analysis: Approximately 321kcal per portion.

LUCINDA GREEN MBE

International Three Day Event Rider, Olympic Silver Medalist

LUCINDA'S PUDDING

Single Cream
Natural Yoghourt
Black grapes - halved and pips removed
Bananas - sliced
Demerara Sugar

1. Mix together equal parts single cream and natural yoghourt.

2. Fold in the halved grapes and the sliced bananas.

3. Place in a shallow heat-proof dish and stand in the refrigerator overnight.

4. Cover with a thick layer of demerara sugar and brown under a very hot grill until the sugar has caramelised.

5. Chill in the refrigerator before serving.

"A very easy recipe which makes an excellent, if fattening, pudding."

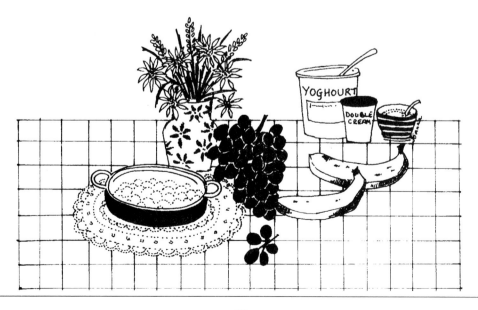

SIR **BRIAN RIX** CBE, DL
Actor, Chairman of MENCAP

MANGO FOOL

2 tins Mangoes
10 fl. oz. Double cream
Grated nutmeg

1. Strain mangoes - sieve.

2. Whip cream and mix with mangoes.   Add a little juice if very thick, sprinkle with nutmeg.

3. Serve, chilled, in individual dishes.

"My favourite quick, delicious, pudding!"

DIANA RIGG CBE
Actress

CARAMEL PEARS

2 oz. Butter
6 tbs Castor sugar
4 Ripe pears, peeled, halved and cored
4 fl. oz. Double Cream
Few drops vanilla essence
2 tbs. Kirsch

1. Melt half the butter in a shallow ovenproof serving dish, large enough to take halved pears in one layer. Sprinkle dish with half the sugar.

2. Place pears cut side down in dish, sprinkle with remaining sugar and top each pear with a piece of butter. Bake uncovered in a hot oven for 20 minutes, basting the pears several times with the pan juice.

3. Mix together cream, vanilla essence and Kirsch. Pour over pears and bake for a further 20 minutes or until cream mixture is thickened.

4. Serve warm, with additional whipped cream.

THE RT HON THE
LORD OAKSEY OBE, JP
Racing Correspondent & Commentator

LORD OAKSEY'S TREACLE TART

For an 8" flan tin:

> ***4 oz. Sweet shortcrust pastry***
> ***(made with plain flour,***
> ***butter, 1 oz. castor sugar***
> ***and mixed with milk).***

For the filling:

> ***4 tbs. Soft white breadcrumbs***
> ***4 tbs. Golden syrup***
> ***1 tbs. Black treacle***
> ***1 tbs. Clear honey***

1. Roll out pastry and line flan tin. Set aside while preparing the filling.

2. Warm the syrup, treacle and honey in a suacepan until runny. Stir in the crumbs and leave to stand for five minutes. Add more syrup if the mixture looks a bit stodgy.

3. Pour into prepared flan case, place on a baking sheet, and bake for 30 minutes in the centre of the oven (375F /190C/ Gas Mark 5).

4. Serve with lots of whipped cream.

   The whole idea is for the tart to be made with as thin a pastry as possible, and for there to be lots of treacly filling.

Helpful hint: When pre-heating the oven pop in the syrup and treacle tins and you'll find they're easier to measure out.

BONNIE LANGFORD
Actress

PAVLOVA

3 Egg whites
6 oz. Castor sugar
1 tsp Vanilla essence
1 tsp Cornflour
1 tsp Vinegar
10 fl.oz. Double Cream
Fruit of the season - Raspberries
Strawberries
Pineapple
Apricots

1. Beat egg whites until very stiff; add sugar gradually. Fold in vinegar and cornflour.

2. Spread mixture on an 8" round of greaseproof paper, placed on a baking tray, making the sides higher than the centre to form a shell.

3. Bake for hour in a slow oven. Cool, remove carefully.

4. Fill with whipped cream and arrange sliced fruit on top.

VIRGINIA BOTTOMLEY JP, MP

CHRISTMAS APPLES

6 Firm cooking apples
4 oz. Mincemeat
6 tbs. Dry white wine
1 Heaped tbs. apricot jam
Icing Sugar

1. Wash the apples, remove the cores. Place in a shallow baking dish.

2. Fill the centres with the mincemeat, and pour over the wine or cider.

3. Bake in a moderately hot oven 375 F/Gas Mark 5 for 30 - 40 minutes, or until soft.

4. Lift the apples carefully from the baking dish, and pour the juices into a saucepan. Add the apricot jam (sieved, if necessary). Stir over a low heat until syrupy.

5. Pour over the apples, and then drench with icing sugar.

6. Decorate each apple with a sprig of holly.

CLIFF RICHARD OBE
Musician

TRANSKEI MUD

1 Tin Condensed Milk
10 fl.oz. Double Cream
7 oz. Digestive Biscuits
Mint Chocolate (Aero or Bitz)

1. To caramelise the condensed milk, boil the tin - unopened and well covered with water - in a pressure cooker for 20 minutes, or in a pan for an hour and a half. Allow to cool over night.

2. Whisk the double cream until it thickens and slowly add the caramelised condensed milk spoonful by spoonful and mix thoroughly. Grate 4 - 6 pieces of mint chocolate into the mixture.

3. Layer in a glass dish with the digestive biscuits, finishing with a cream layer.

4. Place in the refrigerator overnight and sprinkle on grated mint chocolate before serving.

MOIRA SHEARER

Dancer, Lecturer, Broadcaster

BANANA MUCK

"This is wonderfully simple to make. It's really a nursery pudding but I have never yet met a grown-up who didn't demolish at least two large helpings! There's never much conversation if you produce this at a dinner party - just an enjoyable gobbling sound."

1. Whip a pint of double cream until it begins to thicken - but not too much.

2. Peel four, six or eight bananas, depending on size, and, with a sharp knife, slice them VERY FINELY into the cream, stirring carefully until it is nicely thick.

3. Dribble the dark soft sugar here and there over the top - while the pudding chills in the refrigerator the sugar sinks into a lovely treacly pattern.

SIR
KENNETH MacMILLAN
Principal Choreographer to the Royal Ballet, Covent Garden

TIRAMASU

1 Packet sponge fingers
8 tbs. Strong black coffee
2 tbs. Tia Maria
1 Large carton Greek yoghourt
1 Small carton double cream
Few drops of vanilla essence
1 tbs. Sugar
1 tbs. Cocoa

1. Break each sponge finger into three pieces and place in a serving bowl; mix the Tia Maria and the coffee and pour over the broken fingers.

2. Beat the sugar into the yoghourt, add vanilla essence and fold into the lightly whipped double cream.

3. Pour the yoghourt mixture over the sponge fingers, smooth the top and dust with cocoa. Leave to set in the refrigerator for two hours.

"This is a recipe for an Italian pudding that has been "doctored" because of its fattening ingredients. Besides being SWOON MAKING, I feel I am not piling on the calories!"

RACHAEL HEYHOE FLINT MBE

Journalist, Broadcaster, Public Speaker & Sportswoman

HEYHOE FLINT

Danescroft
Wergs Road
Tettenhall Wolverhampton
West Midlands

Telephone: 0902 752103

Dear Jennifer,

I must admit I am a terrible fraud because I cannot cook—
or perhaps do not enjoy cooking therefore can honestly
confess to never really having to make puddings.

I always put our cooking out to tender or Meals on
Wheels; in fact my husband refers to my efforts as
Cordon Noire instead of Cordon Bleu! I have made
one cake in 17 years of marriage and the family
commented that it looked like a volcano and who
helped me lift it out of the oven!!

I suppose my favourite pudding is Cheese and Biscuits;
in order to prepare it I go to Sainsbury's or our
quality grocers in the village of Tettenhall (called
Woodville's) make my purchases, take them out of
the wrappers prior to eating and arrange them
delicately on a cheese board with fresh grapes as
garnish; also add accompanying celery, radish and
carrot sticks.

Seriously all power to your elbow and the cause and I
hope the Cookbook is an enormous success (and please
tell any readers to post under plain cover to me,
any left-overs!!)

Warmest wishes,